Which Woman Are You

Malinia McNeill Woods

Copyright © 2015 Malinia McNeill Woods

All rights reserved.

ISBN: 0990315649
ISBN-13: 978-0990315643

DEDICATION

This book is dedicated to all the women of the world searching for themselves. Please understand that you are fearfully and wonderfully made and know that everything you need to reach your purpose in life is already within.

CONTENTS

Acknowledgments	ii
Dedication	
Meet the Ladies	Pg 1
Janet, The Bossy Woman	Pg 3
Erica, The Needy Woman	Pg 9
Roxy, The Nasty Woman	Pg 16
Mary Ann, The Crazy Woman	Pg 22
Natalie, The Real Woman	Pg 29
Women of the Bible	Pg 34
Which Woman Are You	Pg 75
Bible Women, A Closer Look	Pg 106

ACKNOWLEDGMENTS

Many thanks to my biological sisters and my spiritual sisters for your support and your inspiration. Thank you for helping me to see the beauty that each of us possesses and thank you for recognizing the necessity of the similarities as well as the differences. All glory to God who is the architect of my life who has given me the vision, the drive, and the focus to accomplish His purpose for me.

MEET THE LADIES

Understanding women is a mystery that many have attempted to solve but no one has ever been 100% successful. Just when you think you have figured out exactly what makes women tick something changes and the mystery remains unsolved. When trying to discover who women really are, you must begin by determining which woman you are dealing with. There are 5 distinct types of women that make up the female psyche; the true inner being of a woman. There is the bossy woman, the needy woman, the nasty woman, the crazy woman, and then there is the real woman. There are numerous other characteristics that describe women but these 5 traits encompass practically every facet of women; bossy, needy, nasty, crazy, or real.

Let me introduce you to these 5 women; Janet the bossy woman, Erica the needy woman, Roxy the nasty woman, Mary Ann the crazy woman and Natalie the real woman. As you peer into a typical day in the life of these interesting women, you may see something that reminds you of yourself or resembles someone you know.

JANET

THE BOSSY WOMAN

Janet is a go getter, a hard charger, and a tough business woman. She is well educated; goal oriented, and doesn't let anything or anyone stop her from reaching her destination. When Janet wants something, she does her research, develops her strategy, and carries out her plan. She lives a very orderly life that doesn't have room for spontaneity or impulsive behavior.

The telephone rings and goes to voicemail. "Hello Janet, this is Kevin – Kevin Mathis. We met a few days ago at the fund raiser for the Boys and Girls Club. I hope you don't mind, I got your number from your assistant. I didn't get a chance to talk to you at the fund raiser because you were very busy. I'd love a chance to get to know you. Would you

like to meet for dinner tomorrow night? I hope you can make it. Give me a call at (909) 530-4112. Hope to hear from you.

Goodbye." Janet responded to the voice mail by saying, "my assistant is so fired! How dare she give my home number out to some player who thinks he can just call me up at the last minute and leave a message to ask me out to dinner. He has some nerve. Who asks a person that they haven't even been formally introduced to out to dinner in a voice mail? My calendar is booked months in advance and he thinks he can call me directly and expect me to be available with just 24 hours notice. I don't think so." Janet scans through her calendar on her PDA;

Friday-

    8am – Overseas Conference Call

    9am – Breakfast Meeting

    10:30am – Art Council Presentation

    12:30pm – Project Meeting

    1:45pm – Meet w/Steering Committee

3pm – Complete Reports

7pm – Video Conference Call w/Korea

8pm – After Action Review

9pm – Head Home

"Wow, my schedule is pretty light today. Maybe I can fit in a mani-pedi", Janet surmised.

ERICA

THE NEEDY WOMAN

Erica is a beautiful young lady who has had her share of issues. She was an only child and her parents divorced when she was very young. Her Dad made sure that she had everything that she needed financially and her mom spoiled her with everything money could buy; but both her parents led busy lives that left Erica feeling alone. Erica has been in several long term relationships and each relationship ended primarily the same way and for the same reasons. She was too needy.

"Erica, we can't see each other anymore", Josh stated very matter-of-factly. "For the last few months I've been feeling smothered. It was kind of cute in the beginning when you would called me every few hours to ask what I was doing and tell me you were thinking about me; but after a while, that becomes a problem; especially when you want me to spend ALL my time with you. You're a beautiful woman; you are sweet; and you are kind, but I'm not the type of man that you need". Erica takes a deep breath and then responds as she has so many times before. "What's wrong with wanting to spend time with the man I love? Don't you think it's important to spend time with the one you say you love? If you really love someone, wouldn't you want to be with them?

Wouldn't you want to fulfill

their every need? Wouldn't you want them to know how much they mean to you?" As he walks away, Josh gives Erica one last piece of advice, "Erica, love is more about the quality of the time you spend than the quantity. You need to find a man who can be all that for you. I'm not the one." Tears sting Erica's eyes as she ponders the question; "is there someone for me? Will there ever be someone just for me?"

Which Woman Are You

Malinia McNeill Woods

ROXY

THE NASTY WOMAN

Roxy is loud both figuratively and physically speaking. She says what is on her mind and has absolutely no filter.

Roxy makes her living as an exotic dancer and she needs no stage name. She's sexy without even trying and her confidence is over the top at all times.

When she is on stage, she is the center of attention. When she is off stage, she turns heads everywhere she goes. The tiny outfit she wears onstage leaves little to the imagination. The form-fitting attire she wears off stage is less revealing but still exudes sex appeal and her outspoken manner lets you know exactly what she thinks about every situation.

Roxy walks into the sports bar where she is meeting her girl friends for lunch.

She catches the eye of every person in the place, both male and female, who either want to be her or be with her. When she passes one table where two young men are practically drooling with their eyes locked on her over-sized breasts, she stops in front of them, leans over and whispers, "Yes, they are real". She even does a little shimmy to drive her point home. When she reaches the table where her girl friends are waiting, they just shake their heads. "Roxy, you always make quite the entrance. What did you say to those guys over there", Meagan asked. "I just answered the question I know they were asking themselves"

Roxy stated. "Yes, my boobs are real!" All the girls laughed. "Well, at least you didn't flash them this time" replied Jasmine. "Hey, that only happened one time and it was Marde Gras", Roxy defended. "Yeah, it was Marde Gras alright but we were not in New Orleans; we were in Miami", said Meagan. "Potato – Potato", laughed Roxy.

Malinia McNeill Woods

MARY ANN

THE CRAZY WOMAN

Mary Ann has a few nicknames that are tell-tale signs of her personality.

Some people call her "Loco Maria", "Crazy Mary", "Crack Head Mary" or "Manity Insanity". Each of these nicknames stem from events surrounding Mary Ann's love life. The latest object of Mary

Ann's affection is William Pierce.

After 4 months of dating, William stopped calling; stopped answering his phone and his door; and un-friended Mary Ann on social media. These actions prompted what can only be characterized as a "Mary Ann Episode".

Mary Ann showed up at William's job with a picket sign that displayed a large picture of William along with the message that stated "You can't hit it and quit it William". Mary Ann marched back and forth chanting her message over a bull horn for all to hear. Needless to say, this captured everyone's attention; pedestrians, motorists, William and more importantly, William's boss,

Mr. Morgan. Mr. Morgan promptly asked William what was going on and of course William's response was, "she's crazy".

After about an hour of non-stop marching, chanting and disruptive behavior, Mary Ann was interrupted by two police officers who tried to convince her to leave. "Loco Maria" turned her attention onto the men in blue suggesting that they were a part of the male conspiracy.

Mary Ann was finally carted off in the backseat of the police car when her picket sign ended up making contact with a sensitive part of one of the police officer's anatomy. Yes, Crazy Mary swung her sign and hit the cop in the family jewels! As Mary Ann was being taken down town to the police station, all she could think about was William and hope that he saw her creative display and heard her comments. She also hoped that he would answer her call when she was allowed to make one from jail. Maybe he would come down to the county jail and bail her out. "Is it too much to ask for William to come and get me since this is all his fault" thought Mary Ann.

Which Woman Are You

NATALIE

THE REAL WOMAN

Natalie has it all together. She has a job she loves; she's financially secure; and she knows where she wants her future to take her. Although Natalie is very successful in her career, is a mentor worthy of immolation and is motivated to make a difference in the world; she still feels as if something is missing in her life. Natalie is waiting for Mr. Right. "Dear Diary. It's the end of another week and I feel as if I have accomplished so much. Everything is on track for opening another Wal-Mart in an up and coming neighborhood; we have made great progress in our urban re-development project; my sorority has contributed a great deal of time and money to support this year's charity; and I am in the best shape of my life at 110 lbs of solid muscle. There is only one thing that would make me feel like I am complete and that would be to have someone to share my life with. Why is it so hard to find a good man? I'm a pretty good looking person if I do say so myself. I have a good heart; I don't drink or smoke or run around like a party animal. When will I find the man of my dreams? Oh well; I have to just hang in there until Mr. Right makes a left turn down my street and knocks at my door."

Malinia McNeill Woods

WOMEN OF THE BIBLE

IT STARTS WITH EVE

Now, everyone probably knows a woman who exhibits the traits of the women we have just discussed. It may be difficult to accept that in some way many of us have the same issues; however we are not the only ones. If we search our history we will see many examples of the five traits of women; bossy, needy, nasty, crazy and real. Let's begin our search for examples by taking a look at the oldest source of historical information; the bible.

We don't have to go far in our search of biblical scripture to find an example of a bossy woman. The first book of the bible introduces us to the ultimate bossy woman; Eve. Many have heard the story of the Garden of Eden and how the serpent enticed Eve to eat from the forbidden tree and Eve in turn gave the forbidden fruit to her husband Adam.

Genesis 3:6 When the

woman saw that the fruit of the tree was good for food and pleasing to the eye, and also desirable for gaining wisdom, she took some and ate it. She also gave some to her husband, who was with her, and he ate it."

Now many of you may read this passage of scripture and say that it doesn't sound very bossy to you but look closer and give it some thought. In Genesis 2:16-17, God gave Adam instructions that he could eat from any tree except the tree of the knowledge of good and evil. All indications are that Adam obeyed God until Eve later offered him the fruit from the tree. Personally, I believe that Eve made Adam an offer he didn't dare refuse. Now she must have been pretty bossy if Adam gave in even after getting instructions directly from God Himself!

IT CONTINUES WITH SARAH

If you are still not convinced that bossy women existed in the bible, check out Genesis 16:1-6 and take a look at Sarah the wife of Abraham. Sarah, who had been unable to conceive, was in such a hurry to have a child that she demanded that her husband Abraham sleep with her servant in an effort to obtain a child. I don't imagine that it took a lot to convince Abraham to have sex with a pretty lady but it was still a bossy move on Sarah's part.

After the servant became pregnant, Sarah ironically became jealous, angry, and vindictive. Eventually, Sarah became so bossy that the servant ran away. The servant eventually returned but much later, after the child was born, Sarah displayed her bossy ways yet again and this time she forced the servant and the child to leave for good.

Malinia McNeill Woods

JEZEBEL

The ultimate example of a bossy woman in the bible is none other than Jezebel. Jezebel was an evil Queen who was married to King Ahab. King Ahab was well known for being an evil ruler but Jezebel was even more evil and bossy. 1 Kings 21: 1-14 gives an example of how Jezebel used her bossy, evil ways to set up an innocent man to be stoned to death then stole his land in order to expand their own kingdom. Now that's bossy, but 1 Kings also tells of another example of bossy and evil behavior when Jezebel ordered that all the priests of God be killed so that she could promote her religion of worshiping idols.

HANNAH

Just as there are examples of bossy women in the bible, there are examples of needy women. 1 Samuel 1:10 speaks of a woman named Hannah. Hannah was married to a man named Elkanah who loved her deeply. During biblical times men could have numerous wives and father numerous children. In the case concerning Hannah, she was Elkanah's second wife and she was unable to have children. As important as children were during those times, it didn't matter to Elkanah because he loved Hannah despite her barren state. Hannah, on the other hand, was so needy that she felt she had to have a child and she felt that she didn't measure up to Elkanah's other

wife who had numerous children. I'm sure there are many women out there who feel that they don't measure up even when they are loved to excess.

LEAH

Another example of a needy woman in the bible is Leah. Leah was the oldest daughter of Laban and her father tricked Jacob into marrying her instead of her younger sister Rachel. Jacob had already worked seven years for his soon to be father-in-law for the privilege of marrying Rachel because he loved her so. Once Jacob realized that he had been tricked into marrying Leah, he agreed to work another seven years in order to marry Rachel as well. As I previously stated, in those days it was not uncommon for men to have numerous wives but just imagine the kind of problems that would occur when a man married two sisters! Jacob loved Rachel and hated Leah but he performed his duties as both their husband. Leah gave birth to Jacob's children and thought that this would make him love her. Like many modern-day women, Leah thought that she could win Jacob's heart by being intimate with him. Leah's needy side was reflected in the following scripture:

Genesis 29

³¹ When the LORD saw that Leah was not loved, he enabled her to conceive, but Rachel remained childless. ³² Leah became pregnant and gave birth to a son. She named him Reuben, for she said, "It is because the LORD has seen my misery. Surely my husband will love me now."³³ She conceived again, and when she gave birth to a son she said, "Because the LORD heard that I am not loved, he gave me this one too." So she named him Simeon.³⁴ Again she conceived, and when she gave birth to a son she said, "Now at last my husband will become attached to me, because I have borne him three sons." So he was named Levi.³⁵ She conceived again, and when she gave birth to a son she said, "This time I will praise the LORD." So she named him Judah. Then she stopped having children.

NASTY GIRLS

TAMAR

There are several examples of nasty women in the bible. Tamar had been married twice, widowed twice and left childless. She dressed up like a prostitute in order to trick her father-in- law into having sex with her and subsequently had his child. Now by modern standards this act would be considered borderline incest, however, in biblical times it was expected for the males of a family to marry the widow of their deceased family member and father children on behalf of the deceased. Although Tamar was motivated by her rightful desire to have a child, her methods for getting what she wanted fits the category of the nasty woman. The same could be said of Lot's two daughters who got him drunk and had sex with him so they could get pregnant. This incestuous act was calculating and premeditated as the sisters carried out their plans on two separate occasions.

HERODIAS' DAUGHTER

Another example of a nasty woman of the bible was Herodias' daughter who danced naked for her stepfather, King Herod, in order to get him to kill John the Baptist. Although the daughter carried out the provocative dance, she did so with the encouragement of her mother. I guess you could say that Herodias was playing the role of a madam by promoting her daughter to perform in the way that she did. The mother-daughter team schemed to entice King Herod to the point that he would give them anything. Herodias had already nagged her husband into having John the Baptist arrested because he kept telling her that her relationship with King Herod was unlawful; however she was not satisfied with John the Baptist being in prison;

she wanted him dead.

Matthew 14:3-11

3) Now Herod had arrested John and bound him and put him in prison because of Herodias, his brother Philip's wife,

4) for John had been saying to him; "It is not lawful for you to have her."

5) Herod wanted to kill John, but he was afraid of the people, because they considered John a prophet.

6) On Herod's birthday the daughter of Herodias danced for the guests and pleased Herod so much

7) *that he promised with an oath to give her whatever she asked.*

8) *Prompted by her mother, she said, "Give me here on a platter the head of John the Baptist."*

9) *The king was distressed, but because of his oaths and his dinner guests, he ordered that her request be granted*

10) *and had John beheaded in the prison.* 11) *His head was brought in on a platter and given to the girl, who carried it to her mother.*

Each of these women used their feminine wiles to get what they wanted. Some of the women used sex to give life while others used sex to take life away. I guess you could say that sex was their secret weapon.

DELILAH

There were crazy women in the bible as well. Delilah was a prostitute who used sex to find out the secret to Sampson's strength. You might think that since Delilah was a prostitute she would fit the traits of the nasty woman more than those of the crazy woman. In my opinion the definition of crazy was Delilah using sex on three separate occasions to get the strongest man in existence to tell the secret to his strength and then sell that information to the people who would use it against him. A person would have to be crazy to trick Sampson once but a person would have to be totally insane to do something like that three times!

LOT'S WIFE

Another crazy woman in the bible was Lot's wife. Genesis 19 speaks of the life-altering events that took place in the infamous city of Sodom. The scripture describes the scene in which two angels of God came to the city and were approached by Lot to come into his home for the night because the city was so dangerous and evil. No sooner did the angels enter the home than the men of the city surrounded the house; yelling for Lot to send the angels outside so that they could get to "know them" biblically. No amount of pleading from Lot was able to persuade the mob of men from their evil intentions, not even the fact that Lot offered to give them his own daughters. Ultimately, the angels took charge, struck the mob with blindness and escorted Lot, his daughters and his wife out to harm's way. The angels gave very stern instructions to the family to run for their lives and don't look back or stop anywhere in the valley; otherwise they would be destroyed with the rest of the city. Now, I don't know about you, but if I had witnessed the deeds of the angels that had already occurred, I would follow their instructions to the letter. This is why Lot's wife is categorized as the crazy woman because she did not heed their instructions when she turned around to see what was going on in the city they had just escaped. The end result was that Lot's wife was basically mummified as she was turned into a pillar of salt.

RIZPAH

Many of the actions that we consider crazy nowadays may have been viewed as practical in biblical times.

Such is the case of Rizpah, the concubine of King Saul, who gave birth to two of his sons. Most people have heard of the story concerning King Saul and how David eventually became King after Saul and his son Jonathan were killed in battle. However, people are less familiar with Rizpah and her two sons. Once King Saul was dead the lives of any of his remaining family was also at stake. Rizpah's two sons were killed along with most of Saul's remaining sons and their bodies were hanged in the mountains and left exposed. Rizpah laid a blanket out over a rock and stood guard warding off the animals and braving the elements to keep her sons bodies from being ravaged by prey. The sight of her sons decomposing bodies would be enough to make any mother crazy. Rizpah stayed there until King David finally ordered the bones to be properly buried.

Malinia McNeill Woods

THE REAL WOMEN OF THE BIBLE

ABIGAIL

There are many examples of real women in the bible. 1 Samuel 25 introduces Abigail who was married to a wealthy man named Nabal. His name literally meant "fool" and he lived up to that name by refusing to pay for services that were provided to his servants by the great warrior and eventual king, David. Abigail interceded and used great wisdom by bringing excessive gifts to David's army which in turn persuaded David to spare the lives of her entire community.

RUTH

The book of Ruth gives insight into the life of another real woman for which the book of the bible is named. Ruth was a beautiful Moabite woman whose husband died leaving her and her mother-in-law in dire circumstances.

Ruth stayed with her mother-in-law Naomi (another example of a real woman) and worked hard to ensure their survival. She listened to Naomi's instructions and eventually remarried a very successful man who took care of her and Naomi for the rest of their lives.

MOTHER OF CHRIST

The epitome of a real woman in the bible is Mary the mother of Christ. Imagine the strength and fortitude that would be required for a woman in her time that, for all intents and purposes, was pregnant prior to being married. This had to be a difficult task considering that during that time a woman could be stoned to death for acts deemed inappropriate by society. Mary boldly professed to Joseph, explaining all that had occurred regarding the Immaculate Conception and was strong in the face of all the scrutiny from Joseph, the family and the community. It takes a real woman to be strong in the face of this type of adversity that could be the difference between life and death.

Malinia McNeill Woods

WHICH WOMEN ARE YOU

Now that you have read about the mysteries of women, ask yourself, "Which Woman Are You!" If you are truthful in your analysis of yourself your answer to this question would be that you are the bossy woman, the needy woman, the nasty woman, the crazy woman and the real woman. Yes, each of these traits encompasses what it means to be a real woman. If we each look at ourselves very closely in the mirror we will see Janet, Erica, Roxy, Mary Ann, and Natalie staring back at us.

All women have the capacity to be like Janet; bossy for no apparent reason. This stems from our desire to make things happen and to be in control of what happens. The Janet in each of us wants to be the one responsible for the direction that our lives take. The Janet in each of us is willing to make sacrifices to reach the goals we set for ourselves and our families. The Janet in each of us has a "make it happen" mentality that pushes us to take calculated risks that could yield a significant return on all that we have invested toward reaching our goals of success and happiness. The problem with the Janet in each of us is that she lacks the ability to be flexible. She sees kindness and tenderness as a sign of weakness that can be taken advantage of rather than a strength that could help to mold situations or individuals into something awesome. Janet must find a way to be in charge of her future without being a hindrance to her present. Janet must find a way that she can be in control without being overbearing. She must find a way to achieve her mission and accomplish her goals without becoming a tyrant to people around her and without being hostile toward those she encounters along the way. Janet has to make a mental analysis of her motives, her desires, and her methods. She has to closely examine herself to ensure that her actions are warranted and to further determine the necessity of anything that could be considered overkill. There may be occasions in which assertiveness or aggressiveness is appropriate; however, that should not always be the chosen method of dealing with business or life in general.

All women have the capacity to be like Erica, needy to the point of being unbearable. The Erica in each of us emerges from a place of insecurity that causes us to feel unworthy. The Erica in each of us is afraid that those whom we love will eventually tire of us and walk away if we don't hang on for dear life. Erica has some unresolved issues that need to be addressed at the core before she should even consider beginning any type of relationship. There is a deeper reason for any insecurity that a person may have and the key to getting past those insecurities is to determine the origin. If the insecurity is the result of abandonment issues experienced early in life, then it may be a good idea to confront the source of those issues rather than carrying the burden that grows from unresolved problems of the past.

The Erica in each of us is searching for something, or someone to fill a void that we can't quite identify. The problem with the Erica in each of us is that she fails to recognize her own value. She allows herself to be fueled solely by her feelings and does not take the time to delve deeper into what she really needs or who she truly is. The Erica in each of us needs to begin to take care of herself instead of waiting for others to do so. The Erica in each of us has to set about making her own dreams a reality rather than simply being a part of someone else's dream. The way to accomplish this is to make a conscious effort to stop being afraid of being alone. Erica has to embrace the time that she has to be on her own and see this time as an opportunity for self-improvement and development. Erica has to focus on finding her purpose for existing and set her eyes toward achieving her goals and understanding her purpose. Erica has to realize that it is okay to have doubts about who you are, what you should do or where you should go; but it is not okay to do nothing while you're trying to get your bearings.

Just as all women have the capacity to be bossy like Janet and needy like Erica; all women have the capacity to be nasty like Roxy. Many women won't admit to having a nasty side of their character, but that doesn't change the fact that it exists. The Roxy in each of us is viewable when we finally recognize that beauty and sex appeal goes beyond what we see with our eyes. The Roxy in each of us has confidence that is not contingent upon how we are viewed by others but grows as we push the limits of our comfort zone and realize that we are desirable. The Roxy in each of us knows that sex is something that God created to be enjoyed within marriage as indicated in Hebrews 13:4 and in Proverbs 5: 18-19.

The nasty woman within each of us is essential to our overall happiness and our understanding of the power that we have within our marital relationship.

This power is not to be abused

but it is to be used to strengthen the bond that helps to hold a relationship together. The nasty woman is by no means a perverted person; she is a person who embraces her true nature as a caring and giving individual. She is not inhibited and has no qualms about making her desires known and encouraging her spouse to do the same; however there are limitations to the appropriateness of displaying this side of our character. The nasty woman is important, but she is not the sum total of who we are as women. The problem with the Roxy in each of us is that she forgets that there is more to her than meets the eye. The problem with the Roxy in each of us is that she grows accustomed to being viewed as a symbol of physical attraction and forgets to spend time developing other aspects of her character. The Roxy in each of us has a tendency to get so immersed in our physical appearance that we overlook the value of hard work, dedication, and commitment to moral values and civil behavior. The Roxy in each of us needs to recognize that there is more to life than physical pleasure and there is more to a relationship than satisfying our carnal desires. There is nothing wrong with embracing our sexy side but there should be more to us than that. The difficulty comes into play when we don't know how to change gears when we should. Sex is an important component of marriage but, as we all know, some of us don't wait for marriage to partake in sexual activity. One of the side effects of sex outside of the bonds of marriage is the fact that sex is habit-forming. When people begin to engage in sexual activity outside of marriage it becomes a vehicle that can be used to foster relationships that may not necessarily be good for us. I'm sure there are women out there who can relate to being in relationships that they look back on and wonder why they were ever in them. In many cases the reason the relationship lasted to any extent was that it became sexual. Sex clouds judgment and for that reason it is so important to already know everything you need to know about a person before you engage in sexual activity. If we are honest with ourselves we will admit that we have put up with a lot from our mates because we were being satisfied sexually. That is all the more reason why sex outside of marriage is not a good idea. Our desire should be to be satisfied mentally and spiritually before we are satisfied sexually.

One way to tame the Roxy in each of us is to tone down our appearance and turn down our volume. In no way am I suggesting that we done a habit such as those worn by nuns or take our fashion sense from the

Amish, unless that's your type of style. There's nothing wrong with enjoying yourself and expressing yourself through what you wear; but we should be able to do so without alienating others or causing serious discomfort in the process. What we wear should be a reflection of how we want to be perceived. There is such a thing as being sexy and classy at the same time. We should not take our cues from celebrities or Hollywood images; we should me motivated by how we want to feel and how we want to be viewed. Although it may be tempting to let everything hang out, it is far better to leave some things to the imagination. If a woman feels the need to put herself on display for every eye to see, then she should ask herself the question, why. Why does she feel that it is necessary to wear revealing clothing or practically no clothing at all? What does she think will happen if she dresses more conservatively or in a manner that doesn't draw overt attention to her anatomy? If the answers to either of these questions is that she fears being ignored or feels that she has nothing else to offer, then it's time for a lesson in self esteem. When a woman values herself, she will not feel the need to seek validation from others. When a woman is confident in her own abilities, she will not seek to distract people with an overly sexual persona that is addicted to the attention received as a result of wearing lust-provoking attire. Although wearing "daisy-dukes" will get you noticed by the male population, it's not worth the side effect of a yeast infection.

La vida loca is the Spanish way of saying the crazy life. The Mary Ann in each of us has a way of making our life crazy and interesting at the same time. Mary Ann represents that inner-crazy person that just needs the right kind of situation to appear and raise all kinds of hell. When Mary Ann is unhappy, disgruntled or otherwise upset, Mary Ann switches into turbo and everyone feels the heat.

Mary Ann is not clinically diagnosed as impaired in some way, mentally challenged or psychologically inept. Mary Ann is just a woman at the end of her rope. She has tried to be heard in the typical manner and her cries have either gone unheard, unanswered, or ignored. Mary Ann has been pushed to the edge and has decided to take the plunge which has led to behavior that can be characterized as bazaar to say the least. This characterization in no way suggests that mental illness doesn't exist; however in this case, the issues that Mary Ann has comes as a result of outside stimuli and can usually be traced to something in her love life. Mary Ann is a passionate person who wears her heart on her sleeve and as a result often falls prey to people who do not have the best of intentions. She is an intriguing character who makes people curious about her because of her free spirit and her tendency to go to great lengths to please the people in her life. Mary Ann is creative and uses her creativity in a way that usually ends up making her actions very memorable. If Mary Ann chose to utilize that creativity for a good purpose, she could make a positive impact on her community, her family and society at large.

The problem with the Mary Ann in each of us is that we only know one speed and that speed is fast and furious. When the Mary Ann in each of us decides to love, she does so with everything she has and gives it her all. Unfortunately, Mary Ann can be too much to handle especially when you consider that the relationship has just begun. Mary Ann has to learn to take things slowly. Mary Ann has to purposely allow people to get to know the real her just as she gets to know the real them. The only way to do that is with time and effort. The process cannot be rushed and cannot be demanded. Mary Ann has to learn patience and realize that anything worth having is worth waiting for. Mary Ann has to know that while she is worthy of being loved she cannot force people to love her; she can only show love and know that eventually love will be shown in return.

Now to understand, Natalie, the real woman you have to understand Janet, the bossy woman, Erica, the needy woman, Roxy, the nasty woman and Mary Ann, the crazy woman because all these traits are what makes Natalie, the real woman. Real women get bossy when they feel it's warranted or when they recognize that they are the only ones that can be counted on to help them reach their goals. Real women become bossy when they are being challenged simply because of the fact that they are female or because they are not being taken seriously in their role. Real women become needy when they are overcome by world events or situations that challenge their ideals about who they are, where they are going, or what they are capable of accomplishing. Real women become needy when their strength has been battered to the point of exhaustion and they begin to question their abilities. Real women have a nasty side of them that craves a physical connection to someone who wants to be with them and desires to reach a level of intimacy that can only be described as kismet. Real women also become nasty when they see that their feminine wiles can be a tool for allowing them to get what they want from their relationships. Real women get crazy when they feel that the only way to resolve an issue is to elevate the response level to a magnitude that leaves no room for doubting the serious nature of the offense. Real women also get crazy when their way of life has been challenged in a way that no other course of action seems to be enough of a response and the circumstances are beyond any normal scenario.

Although it may be hard to

imagine, every woman is capable of being bossy, needy, crazy, nasty or real at any given time; including the women of the bible. When we read the bible it is easy to make the assumption that certain women of distinction may be incapable of displaying the character traits that we have been discussing. We visualize biblical women according to their positions or their status and think of these women as one-dimensional; however, close examination will prove otherwise. Let's take a closer look at some of the biblical women we have already discussed.

BIBLE WOMEN
A CLOSER LOOK

We have recognized that Eve, the first woman in the bible was indeed bossy as displayed by her actions in the Garden of Eden; however in my opinion, Eve was also very needy. Think about the incident between Eve and the serpent. Eve ate the fruit and then gave it to Adam for him to eat as well. I believe that Eve offered the fruit to Adam as a result of her need for his support and agreement. Sarah was indeed a bossy woman as displayed by her actions of forcing her husband to father a child with their slave and then eventually forcing the slave and her child to leave; however, Sarah was also needy for those same reasons. She needed a child and was willing to do almost anything to have one but she also needed to be the center of her husband's attention. Jezebel, the ultimate bossy woman was also crazy. How else do you explain a person taking time to put on makeup , fix her hair and put on jewelry when she knew that she was about to be killed!

Just as the previously mentioned bossy women have a needy side and a crazy side; the needy women of the bible also have another side to them. Hannah was definitely needy to the point that she fervently prayed without ceasing year after year in an effort to change her barren state and eventually conceived a child; but she was also bossy. This bossy, firm side of her character was evident when after all those years of petitioning God to give her a child, Hannah vowed to give him back to God by taking him to the temple to live and serve God once he was old enough. Leah was characterized as needy because she saw her ability to be intimate with her husband and give birth to his children as a way to force him to love her but Leah was also a bossy woman. In Genesis 30, Leah showed that bossy side when she brokered a deal with her sister Rachel to force Jacob to have sex with her in exchange for some fruit. Once she had negotiated the terms with Rachel she went to Jacob and demanded that he sleep with her and he obliged. As a result of this sexual encounter Leah conceived her sixth child. Now that was a serious negotiation because I don't know any wife who would allow her husband to have sex with someone else in exchange for something as simple as a few berries.

EPILOGUE

I challenge each of us to search the scriptures and make comparisons between ourselves and the women depicted in the bible. Close examination will allow us to observe the connection that exists and further allow us the opportunity to know more about who we are as well as who we should aspire to be. Knowing who we currently are is an important part of becoming who we are purposed to be. Once we understand that it is okay to be bossy, needy, nasty, crazy and real; we can set our sights on becoming the best of all these character traits combined.

We all are real women and we all have value. The secret to being a real woman is finding that happy medium between bossy, needy, nasty, crazy and real. Our goal should be to successfully balance the scales and find just the right mix of our character traits so that we can be the real women that we each are capable of being. If you are only known as Janet, Erica, Roxy, Mary Ann or Natalie, you still have some work to do but you have all the tools you need to become the real woman that you are destined to be. All it takes is for you to decide which women you truly want to be and set about the business of analyzing where we stand in the grand scheme of things. The answer to the question "Which Woman Are You" is very easy to explain; we are every woman.

Which Woman Are You

About the Author

Malinia McNeill Woods is a retired Army Warrant Officer who is also a mother, a worship leader and a talented song writer. Malinia has a genuine love for humanity and seeks to challenge our thinking while we learn more about whom we are and who we are purposed to be.

www.ingramcontent.com/pod-product-compliance
Lightning Source LLC
LaVergne TN
LVHW051503070426
835507LV00022B/2901